For links to video
clips to hear all the
tunes in this book, go to
www.usborne.com/quicklinks
and type the keywords
"keyboard book".

D1501929

Before you start playing the tunes in this book, have some fun pressing the different notes on the keyboard.

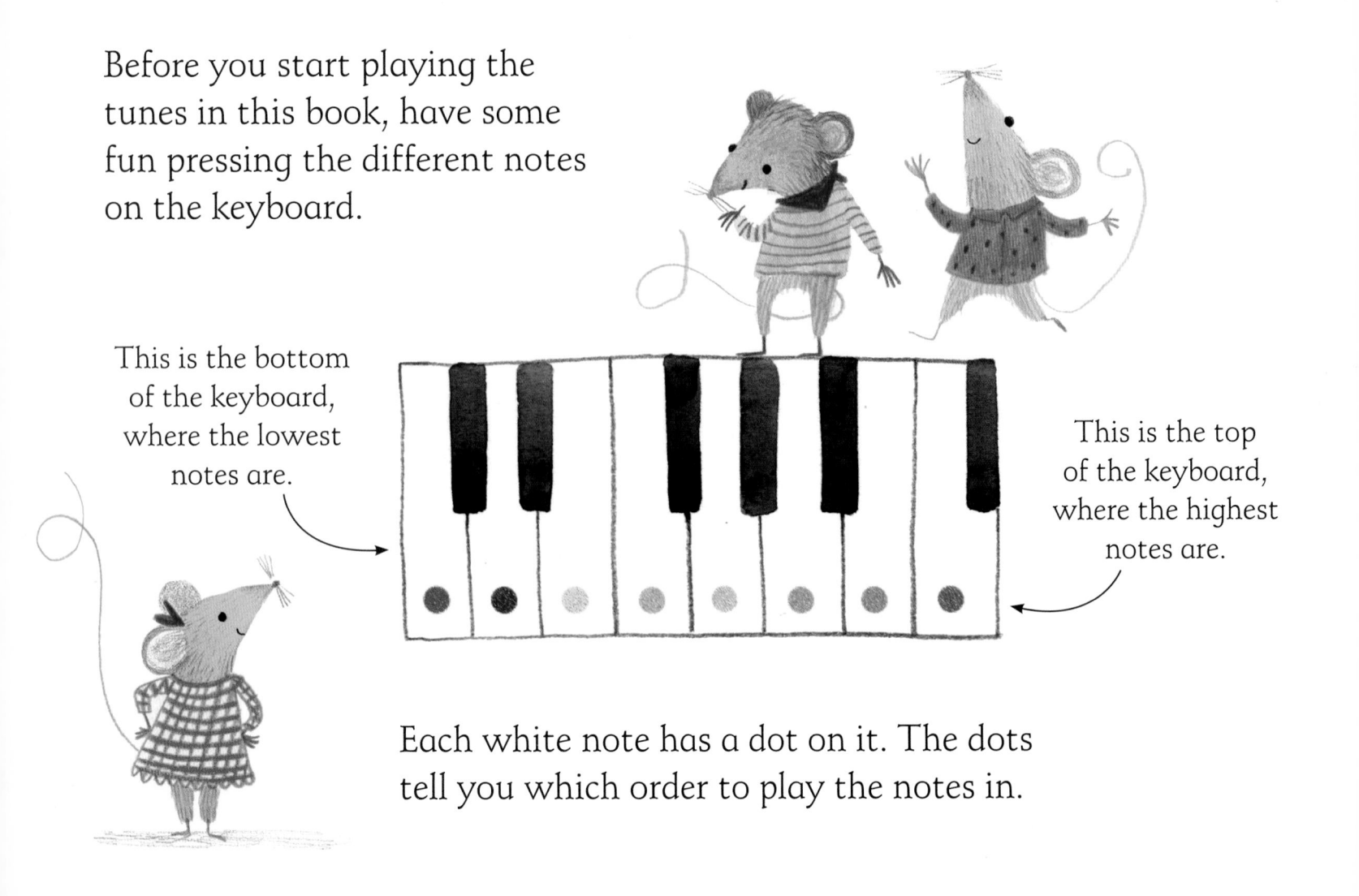

This is the bottom of the keyboard, where the lowest notes are.

This is the top of the keyboard, where the highest notes are.

Each white note has a dot on it. The dots tell you which order to play the notes in.

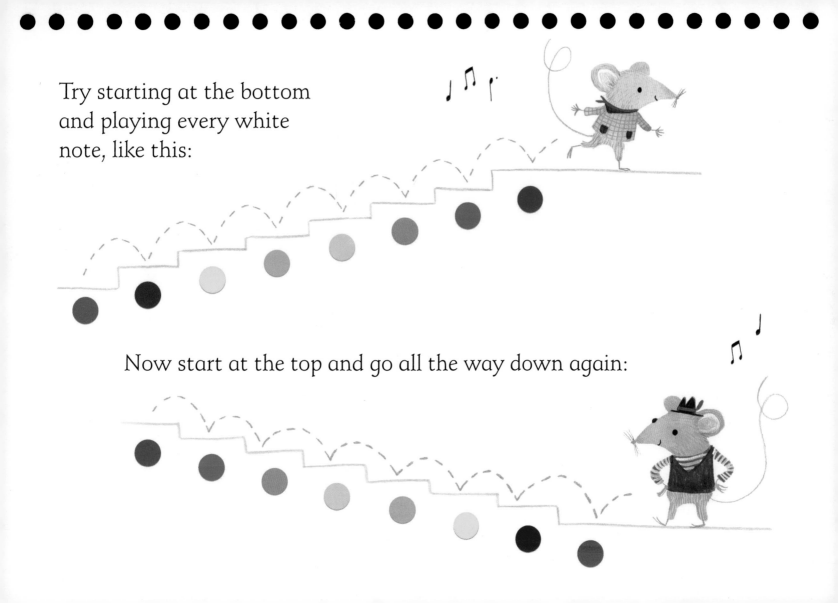

Try starting at the bottom and playing every white note, like this:

Now start at the top and go all the way down again:

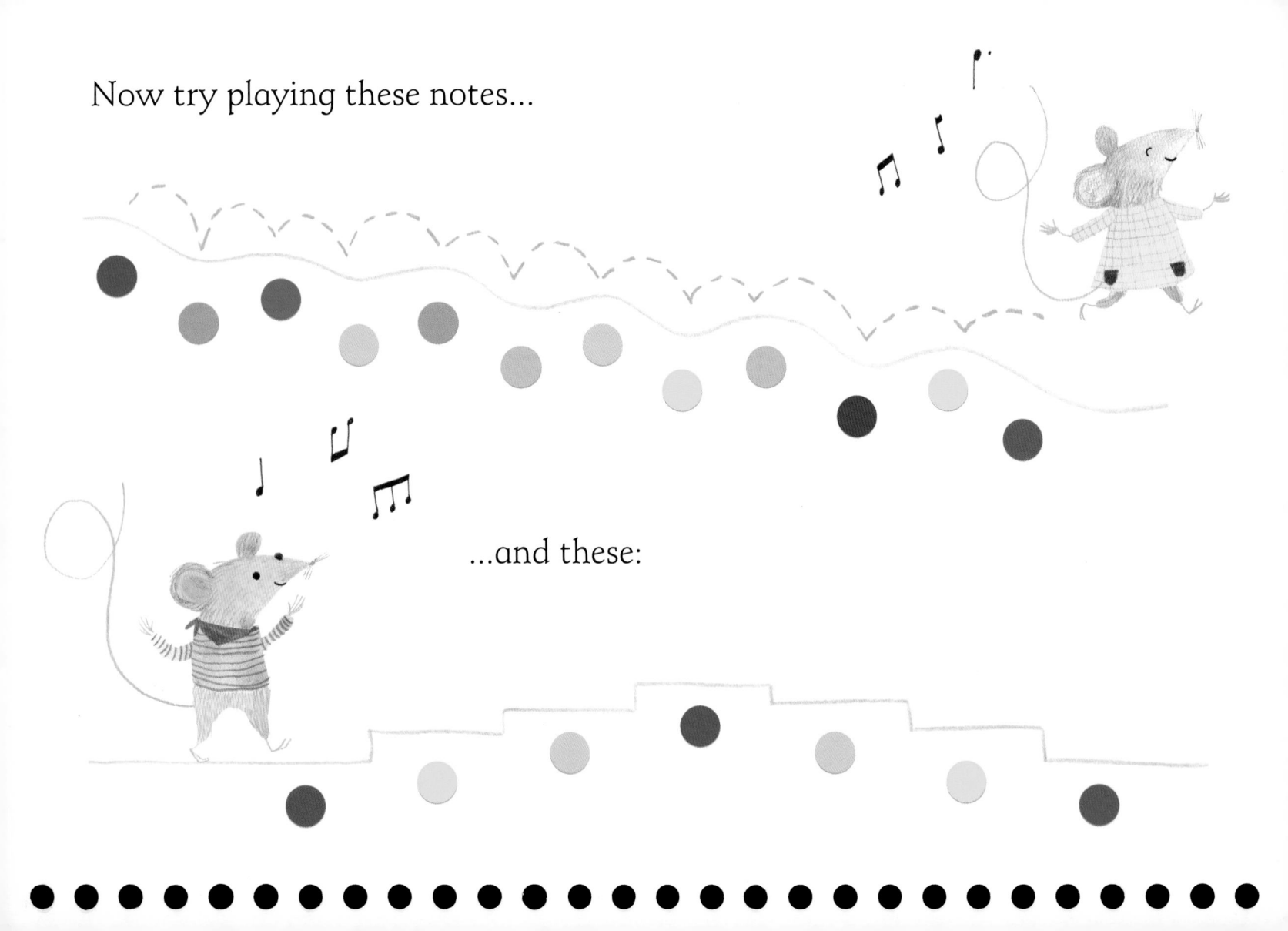

Now try playing these notes...

...and these:

These sets of three notes sound nice when you play them in a row. Can you find more sets of three notes that sound good?

The black notes are fun to play too, though you won't need them for the tunes in this book.

Before you turn the page to learn some tunes, try making up your own by pressing different notes on the keyboard.

Morning

This peaceful tune sounds like the morning sun
rising slowly into the sky. It was written
by Grieg, a Norwegian composer.

Play this tune slowly and gently. Start here.

Ode to Joy

This famous tune is by the German composer Beethoven. It's from his ninth symphony.

This tune is usually sung by a big choir.

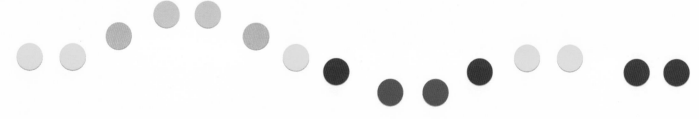

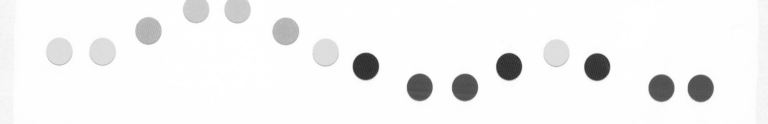

Au Clair de la Lune

This is an old French song. The title means 'In the light of the moon'.

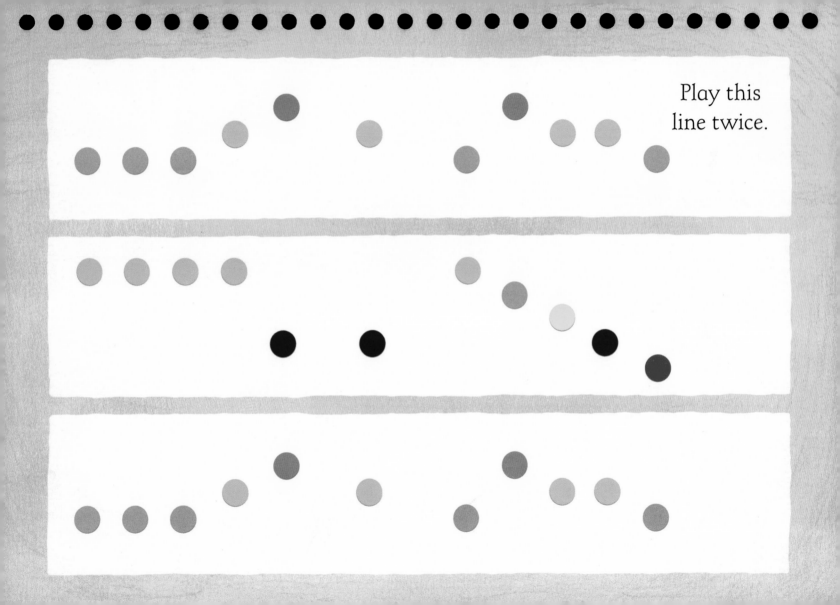

Play this
line twice.

Round the Mulberry Bush

This nursery rhyme is about dancing around
a mulberry bush on a cold and frosty morning.

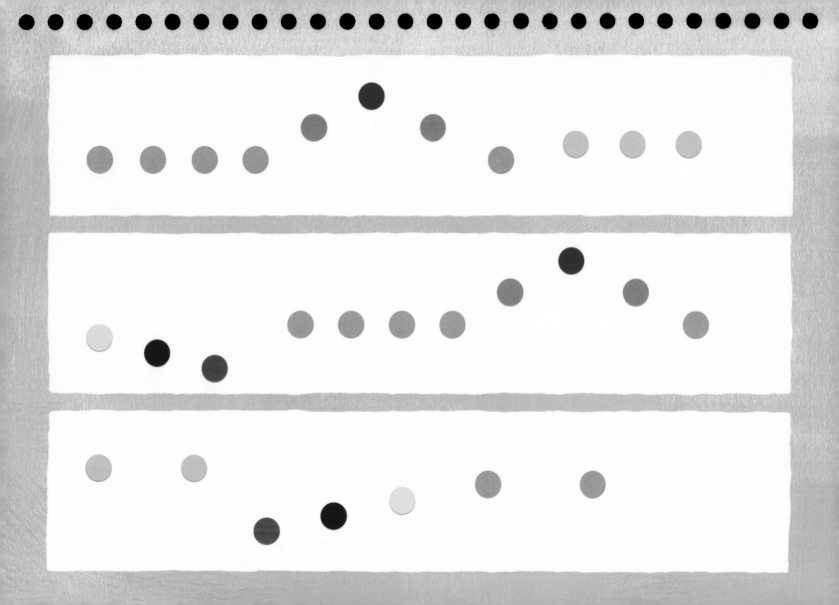

Row, Row, Row your Boat

This tune is from an old nursery
rhyme about rowing a boat along
a stream on a summer's day.

Old MacDonald

This tune is from a traditional song
about all the different animals
on Old MacDonald's farm.

Play this
line twice.

Twinkle, Twinkle, Little Star

This very famous little tune
is from a song about staring
up at a star in the night sky.

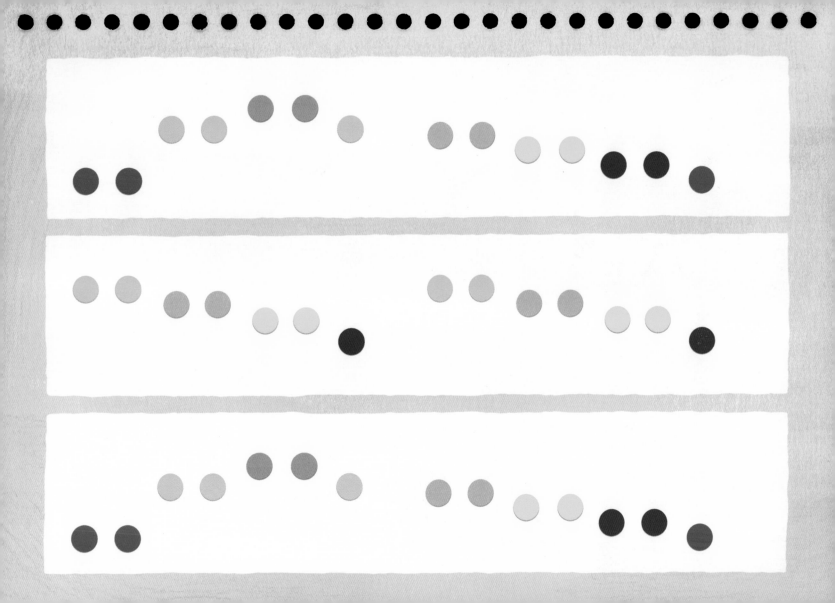

Three Blind Mice

This tune is from a popular nursery rhyme about the adventures of three little mice on a farm.

Play this line
three times.

Frère Jacques

This tune is a French nursery rhyme.
The words describe someone being woken
up in the morning by noisy church bells.